NATIONAL GEOGRAPHIC

T0045528

Seeing Things Up Close

Kate McGough

This is my magnifying glass.
It helps me to see things up close.

I see a ladybug up close.
It has black spots on its back.

I see a butterfly up close.
It has yellow spots on its wings.

I see an ant up close.
It has antennae on its head.

I see a caterpillar up close.
It has stripes on its body.

I like to see things up close.
Do you?